Penguin Modern European Poets
Advisory Editor: A. Alvarez

Selected Poems · Blaise Cendrars

Novelist and poet, Blaise Cendrars was born Frederic Sauser in Switzerland in 1887. According to legend, he escaped his parents' imprisonment at the age of fifteen by swinging down from a fifth-floor balcony, and subsequently lived in Moscow, Peking, New York and Paris. In fact, he was apprenticed to a watch merchant at the age of seventeen, and it is unlikely that he ever went to China. He did lose an arm while serving in the Foreign Legion during the First World War. His spirited nomadic life, where fact and fiction often mingled, inspired many of his marvellously adventuresome and vivid narratives, written with the speed and flexibility of a movie camera. He was the author of more than twenty books, was associated with the Cubist movement, and, along with Apollinaire and Max Jacob, was one of the founders of the modern movement in literature. He died in Paris in 1961.

Blaise Cendrars' masterful novel, *Moravagine*, is also published in Penguins.

Peter Hoida, the translator, is a painter and poet. His published collections of poems are *Lips* and *Stumble*.

Selected Poems

Blaise Cendrars

Translated by Peter Hoida
With an introduction by Mary Ann Caws

 Penguin Books

Penguin Books Ltd, Harmondsworth,
Middlesex, England
Penguin Books, 625 Madison Avenue,
New York, New York 10022, U.S.A.
Penguin Books Australia Ltd, Ringwood,
Victoria, Australia
Penguin Books Canada Ltd, 2801 John Street,
Markham, Ontario, Canada L3R 1B4
Penguin Books (N.Z.) Ltd, 182–190 Wairau Road,
Auckland 10, New Zealand

This selection first published by Penguin Books 1979
Introduction copyright © Mary Ann Caws, 1979

Translation copyright © Peter Hoida, 1979
All rights reserved

Made and printed in Great Britain by
Richard Clay (The Chaucer Press) Ltd, Bungay, Suffolk
Set in Monotype Bembo

Contents

Introduction

> I always see him there in the hub of the universe,
> slowly revolving with the vortex . . . Cendrars is
> the eye of the navel, the face in the mirror which
> remains after you have turned your back on it.
>
> Henry Miller[1]

Cendrars always remembered his old music teacher's saying that life could be accepted only if it were reinvented every day. This seems to have prompted a certain amount of myth-making in his own biography. Frédéric Sauser was born in La Chaux-de-Fonds, Switzerland, and not in Paris, as he sometimes claimed; not of a Scottish mother, but a Swiss one, in 1887. He wrote Freddy Sausey on his schoolbooks, and the penultimate transformation of his name, to Braise Cendrart (ember ash art), was described by his friend Ludwig Rubiner as taking its origin in two lines of Nietzsche: 'Und alles wird mir nur zur Asche/Was ich liebe, was ich fasse.' As for 'Blaise', Cendrars explained that it came from 'Braise', by a simple Chinese-style confusion of the consonants *r* and *l*: but of course the 'Braise' itself may be legend. In the final change from Cendrart to Cendrars we may see as much arson of former and future moments as we choose: we know in any case that the name mattered to him. A story of 1952, found in *Trop c'est trop/Too Much is Too Much* (Denoël, 1957), concludes with the revealing words about his life in the Paris of 1907 as it was reflected on fifty years later: 'To sum it all up, I didn't exist at that point and I'll never be mentioned in

1. In his preface to the New Directions edition of Cendrars's poetry, ed. Walter Albert, 1962.

any history or manifesto because I hadn't yet found my pseudonym: BLAISE CENDRARS.'

After a sporadic series of educational experiences (an English governess, a German gymnasium, a commercial school in Neuchâtel, where he had the distinction of attaining 372 absences in 1901 to 1902), Cendrars spent heavily in bars and displeased his father in still other ways until he was imprisoned with only bread and water in his house; he escaped, taking what silver and money he could, wandered through train stations and met, in Pforzheim, an itinerant jewel peddler named Rogovine who befriended him and took him to Russia and Siberia. So goes the legend; it seems that in fact Cendrars's father apprenticed him to a watch merchant, Leuba, at seventeen. Fact and legend converge: Cendrars was smitten by a Russian girl, Hélène, so that her death permitted him just that sadness he was most to enjoy, finding suffering to be, at that period, 'the essence of my life'. Compare his picture of the ocean as he crossed from St Petersburg to New York in 1911 to rejoin Féla (a Polish student he had met at the University of Berne)[2]: 'Its saddened visage is my own. This horrid unfurling expanse is my bitterness. I too have my abysses.'

It is said that he carried with him trunkloads of books wherever he travelled – and legend has it that this included China, Persia, Egypt and Armenia.[3] Like his ancestors, called 'Humanist vagabonds' by one critic, he retained a passionate curiosity: in Russia, he traced old French books; in Czechoslovakia, he read vast quantities of material on Rosicrucian trials. In 1907 he kept

2. Myriam Cendrars, Féla's daughter, is now bringing out the unpublished manuscripts of her father. The *Inédits* include, for instance, the partial manuscript on perspective quoted here.

3. He probably went neither to China nor to Persia. See the *Inédits secrets*, ibid.

bees, in 1908 he is said to have been a juggler in the music halls of London with Charlie Chaplin, in 1909 he was a tractor driver in Winnipeg. But the volume of *Inédits secrets* challenges this entire series of stories.[4] In 1912, during a period of intense financial stress in New York, Cendrars says he wrote his most famous poem, 'Pâquesà New York' (Easter in New York), whose unpunctuated couplets came to him, he continues, in a night of walking through the snow after a performance of Haydn's *Creation*. When Cendrars read them to a group of friends including Apollinaire in Paris, the latter is said to have removed the punctuation from his own even more famous 'Zone', which however he eventually published with earlier poems, as if it had been composed in 1898. (Tristan Tzara, who kept the manuscript, verified this tale.) In Paris, Cendrars was particularly close to Robert and Sonia Delaunay, to the simultanist-futurist-orphic group gathered around them, and to the poets and painters associated with the Bateau Lavoir. Eventually he enlisted in the Foreign Legion and lost his right arm at the front in the Champagne offensive of 1915: thus the title of one of his autobiographical books: *La Main coupée* (*The Severed Hand*).

His travels and varied professions (including publishing, as an editor of the Éditions de la Sirène in 1918) continued ceaselessly, re-imagined and recounted in his unmistakable prose-poems and novels in their odd mixture of simultaneous narration and self-contemplation. Since Cendrars believed, as he tells us in *Mora-*

4. Including the Charlie Chaplin episode, and the Winnipeg adventure of 1909. He seems to have made only one trip from St Petersburg to New York in 1911, staying in the latter from 11 December to 12 June; but he read travel magazines with great avidity. (My thanks to Monique Chefdor for enlightenment on the thorny problems of legend and fact and for the material in footnotes 3, 5, 7.)

vagine (which can be translated roughly and misogynistically as death to the vagina), that equilibrium is the first obstacle to freedom, he maintained himself in constant flight from the static attitude he discerned in the artificialities and conformism of most writers' lives. He preferred a conglomeration of 'feverish, multiple, risky activities ... Poetry in action'. But life is renewed by contrasts, he said, and his writing is always disposed between two opposite poles, characterized by the statements: 'I don't like to lose my directions', and 'I like my lucidity. It's my lucky star.' (*L'Homme foudroyé*/*The Stricken Man*). Like the Brahmin in reverse to whom he compares himself, he was always observing, even in the midst of the most arduous adventures, so that the action is always doubled by a contemplation of that action.

An intense visual impulse infects Cendrars's style, which is actively presentational rather than passively descriptive, immediate rather than contemplative. Above all other art forms, he preferred, as we would have been able to predict, the cinema. With Abel Gance in 1920 to 1921, he filmed *La Roue* (*The Wheel*) in which the train sequence is strongly reminiscent of his own masterpiece, *La Prose du Transsibérien*; prose, he said, because 'Poem' was less modest and less common. (The sequence was set to music by Arthur Honegger in a tone-poem, 'Pacific 231'.) Two films were made of his popular novel *L'Or*, subtitled 'the wonderful story of General Johann August Suter', one of his ancestors with whom he vicariously identified: see the long poem 'Le Panama ou les aventures de mes sept oncles'. Cendrars's enthusiasm for the cinema is described in the essay 'Profond aujourd'hui' ('Deep Today'); the idea of depth includes, for him, the rhythmical as well as the intense, both qualities he chose in his own life and its alternations of careers and voyaging. To both the life and the art, he could apply the definition: 'a whirlwind of moments in space'. Cendrars explained that he had wanted in all his work to suppress the notion of ordinary time as serial and to validate that of simultaneous action – preferring the relativity of Einstein in his composition, and the technique of Bach in his execution.

Abel Gance praised his simplicity and spontaneity in displaying his 'interior riches' in the making of films, but since, as Cendrars admitted, he had no real practice in the métier, his final experience with his own film company in Rome was not a success.[5] From 1926 to 1927, he was in Latin America, where the tales of his speeding about with his one hand on the wheel of his Alfa Romeo are a further if trivial testimony to his constant rapidity of movement in all areas of living. In the Second World War he was a correspondent attached to the English army; the record of his experiences, *Chez l'armée anglaise*, was destroyed by the Germans after the invasion. As his home at Tremblay-sur-Mauldre had been pillaged, he settled with his wife Raymone in Aix-en-Provence, growing medicinal herbs and working in the Méjanes Library on his research into the life of St Joseph of Cupertino, an Italian monk of the sixteenth century, patron saint of aviators (who had levitated at least seventy times, according to the account of his biographer Olivier Leroy). From Cendrars's work on that saint, *Le Lotissement du ciel* (*The Parcelling of the Sky*) – a sort of prose poem to vertical movement – comes the following image of writing, notable for its insistence on depth and on light:

Writing is to descend like a miner to the depths of the mine with a lamp on your forehead, a light whose dubious brightness falsifies every-

5. The story runs that he made a last film, on elephants in Africa, but this story may be due to association with the poem 'Elephant Hunt', inspired, according to T'Serstevens, by a Belgian travel book on the Congo.

thing, whose wick is in permanent danger of explosion, whose blinking illumination in the coal dust exhausts and corrodes your eyes.

But that interior mine went untouched for three years after the discouragement provoked by the war; then the metaphor of *braise* and *cendres*, embers and ashes, returns as the myth of the fire is rekindled. His statement is the most pertinent we have on his choice, not only of a name, but of a life:

> For writing is to consume oneself ... Writing is a fire which lifts on high a great confusion of ideas and conflagrates groups of images before reducing them to crackling embers and falling ashes. But the spontaneity of the fire remains mysterious. For writing is burning alive, but is also to be reborn from ashes.

Cendrars died in Paris in 1961 after a bout of hemiplegia and a partial paralysis. 'I shall have been one of the first poets of my age to have determined to live my life on a worldwide scale,' he said.

*

The tension between two concepts, of outer and inner life, of 'systole and diastole', construction and destruction, optimism and pessimism, is not only examined in Cendrars's 'meta-physical' novel *Dan Yack*, but exemplified in his way of being and of seeing.[6] His most vital statements concern his self-observation, as he was 'contemplating himself in agitation, keeping in constant training and scorning life with all his strength.' In this case the reader has not to choose between a study of the man and a study of the text, for the latter makes no pretence of being more than a transcription of Cendrars's often deliberately naïve

6. It is perhaps worth noting, as Walter Albert does in his translations of Cendrars, that from 1913 to 1924 Cendrars wrote his poems, and after 1924, his novels. There are thus two poles even in the literary production.

14

relation to the world about him, a scene to which he accords an importance exactly equal to that of his own being: 'For the loftiest passion is the passion of oneself, in complete sincerity.' Contemporary art, he said, is meant to show the 'naked interior man', but paradoxically, the latter seems graspable only in his enthusiastic turning towards the rapid motion of exterior reality – thus the frequent images of express trains, airplanes, and all the vehicles of motion.

In an extraordinary manuscript on perspective, published with the other 'inédits', and dedicated to the painter Fernand Léger, Cendrars contrasts the mechanistic manner of seeing separate parts of objects, each brightly illuminated and in perspective – a viewpoint we might compare with the classical as Wölfflin determines it – and the vitalistic or modern viewpoint in which the spectators are never immobile as they would be in perspectival art, moving as they are with the spectacle. Here one image replaces another or is linked to many others, all merged in a 'crowd of hurried images, pushing and shoving each other. What was once a solid and fixed object is swept away in a future spilling over into a thousand correlations, a thousand relationships, a thousand repercussions.' Thought surrounds life, as the interior subjectivity upsets the spatial order of perspective, forcing on all Cendrars's own writing – whether novelistic, poetic, or critical – this disquieting dynamism. 'Everything around me moves.' But the paradox of writing life as opposed to living was disturbing to him. In an article of 1913, published in *Der Sturm*, Cendrars declares:

I have a taste for risk. I'm not a man to be closed in. I've never known how to resist the call of the infinite. Writing is the thing most contrary to my temperament and I suffer damnably at being shut up between four walls and blackening paper when life is stirring outside, when I hear the car horns on the road, train whistles, the sirens of ships, and I think of the lost lands I do not yet know . . .

Cendrars's reaction to the world about him is based on the same spirit as Apollinaire's line: 'Crains qu'un jour un train ne t'émeuve plus.' The world is to be surveyed from as many look-out points as possible and in as wide a scope; oceans, islands and continents are glimpsed in moving perspective, from the privileged space of a ship's deck or a train window, like that of the Transsiberian Express, in honour of which Cendrars created 'The First Simultaneous Book', with Sonia Delaunay's brightly-coloured disks alongside his poetry. In this epic and yet simple poem, the traveller's companion asks again and again: 'Dis, Blaise, sommes-nous loin de Montmartre?/Tell me, Blaise, are we far from Montmartre?' as they hurtle through country after country, whose landscapes are catalogued and transposed in the poet's imagination, free of category and hierarchy, never to be separated from the interior world: *Du monde entier* as a title leads to *Au coeur du monde* (*From the Whole World* to *The Heart of the World*), showing the same deliberate contrast as the single title: 'La Prose du Transsibérien et de la petite Jehanne de France'.

*

Cendrars's poetry is, as has often been said, a poetry of simultaneity. Simultaneous has here at least two senses: the writing in its immediate form occupies the same moment as the visual perception, so that representation is ideally free of afterthought, and the elements of the landscape in their various sizes and apparent importance are presented in identical scale and stress. There are neither differentiations of value nor of time: thus the impression of a chosen lack of forethought, of a chosen naïveté. This, together with the catalogue and collage techniques and Cendrars's close personal association with the cubist poets and their friends Apollinaire, Jacob, and Reverdy ally him to cubism, whereas the direct and unjudging representation of the seen, and the poem considered as a snapshot free of analysis or synthesis, a poetic *cinéma vérité*, lead to the consideration of a new genre. When the Eastman Kodak company protested at the title he had given to one of his collections, 'Kodak', he called them 'Documentaires', since he considered these verbal photographs a document.[7] 'Poetry is not in a title but in a fact', he said. 'We must purge ... all poets and all writing of any setting ... reduce all books to a few pages, essential and bare, to discover what I call '*cosmic lyricism*'.

Cendrars wanted the 'windows' of his poetry to be thrown wide open, like the windows of Apollinaire's poetry. In fact, even the superb brevity of the *Dix-neuf poèmes élastiques* (*Nineteen Elastic Poems*) stretches to cover an astonishing amount of space. The title of the collection echoes that of a painting by the Italian Futurist Boccioni, called 'Elasticità', dating from only one year before the writing of most of these poems, which in fact put into practice many of the tenets of the Futurist Manifestos. The futurist look, like that of the simultanist, is meant to take in several regions of perception at once, offering them together as the multiplicity of views necessary to any object. Robert Delaunay's presentation of fifteen views of the Eiffel Tower within his one greatest painting of it is the perfect image for the attitude,[8] which must include motion and finally equates

7. On the subject of collage techniques, the poems from *Documentaires* have their source in Gustave Lerouge's *Le Dr. Cornelius*. See Lacassin, *Le Magazine littéraire* (no. 9, Juillet–Août 1967), 'Quand la poésie copie le feuilleton'.

8. Cendrars recounts that in 1911 alone, Delaunay did over fifty paintings of the Eiffel Tower before finding the one he liked best. It might

it not only with depth, but with truth, and above all, with passion.
For example, the poem 'Aux 5 coins' (In the Five Corners), as if
four corners of the world were not enough for this exuberance:
'Oser et faire du bruit/Tout est couleur mouvement explosion
lumière/La vie fleurit aux fenêtres du soleil' ('To dare and to
make noise/Everything is colour movement explosion light/Life
flowers at the windows of the sun'). The passion of self to which
Cendrars refers calls for a language sufficiently ardent to convey
the excitement of constant change and sufficiently clear to
observe it.

Cendrars's sensitivity to the exterior world was unembarrassed
and even sentimental. Henry Miller called his world a 'shining
poetic mass dedicated to the archipelago of insomnia'. The
documentary was always to be infused with the most ardent
and wakeful subjectivity and with a morality dependent on the
aesthetic of motion, but also on the awareness of each moment.
Cendrars has something of Watts-Dunton's 'poetics of wonder'
in his make-up, some impulse to value the passing for its
ephemerality. In this setting we might consider one of his war
stories, in which his unabashed contact with a simple and tiny
animal yields its full potentiality in simultaneous self-observation:

I remember that when we reached the crest of the hill at Vimy, a lark
was trilling. I stopped in my tracks ... to hear the bird singing. It re-
mained suspended in the air at a stone's throw from me. The bullets
flying and the shrapnel and the mortars and machine-guns battering all

---

be of interest to compare Robert Delaunay's views on Simultanism, as
described in a letter from Cendrars to André Salmon: 'There is motion.
Everything is colour in motion, depth. We shall find the métier which can
aid a new representative aestheticism. Simultaneous contrasts, comple-
mentary to each other, and synchronic dissonances. Constructive colour is
the métier in all the presentations of the new art.'

spun an invisible cage around it. The lark fluttered its wings and continued singing. I smiled, dazzled. They were trills of love. Springtime.

As the moment takes on its importance for the poet, seemingly out of proportion to the trivial object of perception, the sentences grow shorter until the final word which sums up the preceding images: this characteristic crescendo in tone, developed by a *ritardando* in rhythm and a corresponding reduction in verbiage, is stylistically comparable to a train slowing down rapidly, but whose potential strength is quadruply sensed; the surrealist images of the train stopped at full speed as it hurtles into a virgin forest, or trembling at its momentary departure in a station, these images of a beauty to be 'convulsive' or not to be, produce the same effect on the reader.

Cendrars always identified a 'state of thought' with a 'state of style', and his own style, at once choppy and lyric, forceful and hypnotic, is startling, particularly in certain moments of the novels, where the narration gives way to a prose poem resembling nothing so much as a meditation, or a contemplation of one chosen detail. As for the poems, they are alternately brilliant (especially the terse 'elastic' poems) and flat (the majority of the *Documentaires* and the *Feuilles de route*), but are usually a peculiar mixture of the general and the detailed, the depicted and the sensed, the neutral observation and the emotionally-charged reflection. In the present choice alone, they will be seen to take many forms, from rhymed couplets to telegraphic monosyllables; they are instantly recognizable by their seemingly unplanned structure, their vivid informality. Seen as elements of a documentary, the shots in their motion from one to another, their kaleidoscopic change, have more formal interest than novelty of content. The poems included here extend in subject matter from Negro art and the art of Marc Chagall to a panorama of the United States – which itself extends from a Black Virgin in a ruined California church and the moss of a deserted house near the Golden Gate to the birches and harvests of New England, to the South with its bull-frogs croaking and a black carriage driver asleep, his mouth open and sweat beading on his face while flies swarm about. The alphabet of the world beyond the library is worth reading, and so all the elements enter on the same level – the contents of the poet's suitcase in his ship cabin, the wood telephone poles of Brazil replaced by Pittsburgh steel, calm water and corals, jellyfish and sea urchins, and seagulls wheeling about on a radiant morning.

We are not allowed to forget the poet or his personality: while other shipboard passengers are in evening dress, he wears a seablue suit, corresponding to the elements and not to society; when the other passengers sleep, he is on deck unclothed in the early morning, keeping the sunrise to himself, whereas they would describe the sunset. Sending an 'ocean-letter' instead of a poem, inserting his present weight into his texts of the common-place object ('I come out of the drugstore . . . I weigh my 192 pounds . . . I love you'), taking a simple joy in his own simplicity of expression – these compose a fitting behaviour for what Apollinaire called the era of surprise. Even the touchingly banal is granted the status of the colourful: stars in a black sky above a black water, seen from the ship on what is flatly termed a 'starry night', or those same stars 'softened' after a succession of un-exceptional nocturnal sounds, or a celestial radiance mixed with the sentimental, as stars seen in Paris are said to illumine the poet 'like Raymone, close up'. By day Cendrars describes the Brazilian landscape glaringly varnished by the sun, the fields turned blue by the sky, whereas in France, he says, they would be yellow and white. From the train he writes of the red earth harbouring its dark-green vegetation, from the ship, of the blue sea frothing white. 'There are patches of colour everywhere', he exclaims, and calls for a brilliant-coloured word to transcribe them: 'We don't want to be sad any longer.' To be sure, this is the early Cendrars, the writer of poetry. Later, he wrote only novels and the colours change. But always, in the landscape on which he opened his windows, he included himself, in a total involvement and with a total passion. 'That's why I never lend myself', he said in his autobiographical *Vol à voile* (*Sail Flight*), 'but give and distribute myself freely.'

Finally, in the vital rhythm Cendrars constantly chose, the passion of the 'naked interior man' included also – as in the widest sense of the term simultaneous – the passion of the exterior world and its motion, and of poetry itself. 'All life is only a poem, a movement. I am only a word, a Logos, a depth in the wildest, most mystical, most living sense . . .'

Suggestions for Further Reading

compiled with the help of Professor Monique Chefdor

(unless otherwise specified the place of publication is Paris)

Blaise Cendrars, *Oeuvres complètes*, Le Club français du livre, 1971
Blaise Cendrars, *Du monde entier*, Poésie Gallimard, 1968
Blaise Cendrars, *Au coeur du monde*, Poésie Gallimard, 1968
Mercure de France, Blaise Cendrars, No. 1185, May 1962
Cendrars romancier, L'Icasothèque, No. 4, Minard, 1977
Blaise Cendrars, *Poètes d'Aujourd'hui*, préface Louis Parrot, Seghers, 1948
Jacqueline Chadourne, *Blaise Cendrars, Poète du cosmos*, Seghers, L'Archipel, 1973
Hommage à Blaise Cendrars, Institut français de Florence; Rome, Éditions de Luca, 1961
Dîtes-nous, *M. Blaise Cendrars*, ed. by Hughes Richard, Éditions Rencontre, Lausanne, 1969
Blaise Cendrars, *Inédits secrets*, presentation de Myriam Cendrars, Le Club français du livre, 1969
Blaise Cendrars, *Selected Writings*, edited and translated by Walter Albert, New Directions, New York, 1962
Mary Ann Caws, *The Inner Theatre of Recent French Poetry: Tzara, Péret, Cendrars, Artaud, Bonnefoy*, Princeton University Press, Princeton, N.J., 1972
Monique Chefdor, translator and editor, *Postcards from the Americas*, University of California Press, 1976
Europe, Cendrars issue, No. 566, June 1976
Henry Miller, 'Tribute to Blaise Cendrars' in *The Wisdom of the Heart*, New York, New Directions, 1941, pp. 151–8
Henry Miller, 'Blaise Cendrars' in *Books in my Life*, New York, New Directions, 1952, pp. 58–80
Jean Rousselot, *Blaise Cendrars*, Témoins du XXe Siecle, Éditions Universitaires, 1955

A. T'Sertevens, *L'homme que fut Blaise Cendrars*, Denoël, 1972

Some recent scholarly publications
Jay Bochner, *Blaise Cendrars, Discovery and Re-Creation*, University of
  Toronto Press, 1978
Jean Carlo Fluckiger, *Au coeur du texte, essai sur Blaise Cendrars*, Á la
  Baconnière, Payot, 1977
Mario Richter, *La quête du logos et la quête du mythe: Baudelaire, Rimbaud,
  Cendrars, Apollinaire*, A la Baconnière, Neuchatel, 1976
Yvette Bozon Scalzitti, *Blaise Cendrars ou la Passion de l'écriture*, L'Age
  d'homme, Lausanne, 1977

The translator would like to thank
Michele Bosc and Mark Balakdjian
for their kind assistance.

from

Nineteen Elastic Poems

3. Contrasts

The windows of my poetry are wide open onto the boulevards
    and in its shop windows
Shining
The jewels of light
Hear the violins of limousines and the xylophones of linotypes
The ladler washes himself in the towel of the sky
Everything is splashes of colour
And the hats of passing women are comets in the fires of
    evening

Unity
There is no more unity
Now all the clocks show 12.0 p.m., after having been put back
    ten minutes
There is no more time
There is no more money
In the Chamber of Deputies
They spoil the marvellous elements of raw materials

At the bistro
The workers in blue overalls drink red wine
Every Saturday wild-chicken
Gambling
Betting
From time to time a gangster passes in a car
Or a child plays with the Arc de Triomphe
I advise Mr Pig to lodge his protégés in the Eiffel Tower

Today
Change of proprietor
The Saint-Esprit retails himself to the smallest shop-keepers
I read with delight the strips of calico
Coloured poppy red
Only the pumice stones of the Sorbonne are never in bloom
The sign of the Samaritan ploughs down the Seine
And toward Saint-Séverin
I hear
The persistent ringing of trams

It rains electric light bulbs
Montrouge Gare de l'Est Métro Southbound pleasure boats
    people
Everything is a halo
Profundity
Rue de Buci they shout 'L'Intransigeant' and 'Paris-Sports'
The aerodrome of the sky is now, glowing, a painting by
    Cimabue
While in the foreground
Men are
Long
Black
Sad
And smoking, factory chimneys

4. 1. Portrait

He sleeps
He is awake
Suddenly he paints
He takes a church and paints with a church
He takes a cow and paints with a cow
With a sardine
With heads, with hands, with knives
He paints with a cosh
He paints with all the dirty passions of a little Jewish town
With all the aggravated sexuality of the Russian provinces
For France
Without sensuality
He paints with his thighs
He has his eyes on his arse
And it's suddenly your portrait
It's you reader
It's me
It's him
It's his fiancée
It's the corner grocer
It's the cow-herd
The midwife
There are tubs of blood
They wash the new-born there
Skies of folly
Mouths of modernity
Corkscrew-spiral tower
The hands
The Christ
The Christ it's him

He has passed his childhood on the Cross
He commits suicide every day
Suddenly he paints no more
He was awake
Now he sleeps
He strangles himself with his tie
Chagall is surprised to be still alive

10. Latest News

'Oklahoma, 20 January 1914'
Three convicts get revolvers
They kill their gaoler and seize the keys of the prison
They rush out of their cells and kill four guards in the courtyard
Then they seize the young prison shorthand typist
And climb into a carriage which was waiting for them at the
    gate
They leave at full speed
While the guards discharge their revolvers in the direction of
    the fugitives
Some guards leap on horses and dash off in pursuit of the
    convicts
Shots are fired from both sides
The young girl is wounded by a shot fired by one of the guards

A bullet kills the horse which was pulling the carriage
The guards can approach
They find the convicts dead their bodies riddled with bullets
Mr Thomas, ex-congressman who was visiting the prison
    congratulates the young girl

Telegram poem copied from 'Paris-Midi'

January 1914

11. *Bombay Express*

The life I have led
Hinders me from suicide
Everything springs up
Women roll under the wheels
With great cries
The fan-tailed see-saws are at the gates of stations
I have music at my finger-tips

I never liked Mascagi
Neither art nor Artists
Neither gates nor bridges
Neither trombones nor trumpets
I know nothing anymore
I don't understand anymore . . .
This caress
Which makes the geographical map shiver

This year or the next
Art criticism is as stupid as esperanto
Brindisi
Good-bye good-bye
I was born in this town
My son too
Whose forehead is like his mother's vagina
There are thoughts which jolt the buses
I no longer read the kind of books you only find in libraries
Nice ABC of the world

Bon voyage!

Let me take you
You who laugh at vermilion

April 1914

17. Mee Too Buggi

Like the Greeks we believe that any well-educated man should
    pluck the lyre
Give me the fango-fango
Which I apply to my nose
A sound sweet and grave
From the right nostril
There are descriptions of landscapes
Accounts of past events
Reports from far away countries
Bolotoo
Papalangi
The poet among other things describes animals
Houses are bowled over by enormous birds
Women are over-dressed
Rhymes and measures bereft
If one will excuse the exaggeration
The man who cuts off his own leg succeeds in being funny in a
    simple way
Mee low folla
Mariwagi beats the drum at the entrance of his house

July 1914

from

Negro Poems

Big Fetishes

I

A vein of hardwood
Two embryonic arms
The man tears open his belly
And adores his erect member

II

Whom are you threatening
You who go
Arms akimbo
Hardly upright
Just beyond swelling?

III

Nuts of wood
Head in the form of a prick
Hard and refracted
Face blank
Young god unsexed and cynically hilarious

IV

Envy has gnawed your chin
Cupidity lures you
You straighten up
That which your face lacks
Renders you geometric
Arborescent
Adolescent

V

Here are the man and the woman
Equally ugly, equally naked
Him less fat than her but stronger
Hands on their bellies and mouths like money-boxes

VI

She
The bread of her sex which she bakes three times a day
And the full waterskin of the belly
Pulling
On the neck and the shoulders

VII

I am ugly!
Due to sniffing the odour of girls in my solitude
My head swells and my nose will soon fall off

VIII

I wanted to flee the chief's wives
My head was smashed by the stone of the sun
In the sand
There's nothing left but my mouth
Open like my mother's vagina
And it cries

IX

He
Bald
Has nothing but a mouth
A member which reaches his knees
His feet cut off

X

This is the woman I love most
Two intense wrinkles round a mouth like a funnel
A blue forehead
White on the temples
And a look polished like a copper

British Museum
London, February 1916

from

Documentaries

III. *Amphitryon*

After dinner served in the wintergardens among masses of
    lemon trees jasmins and orchids
There is a ball on the lawn of the illuminated park
But the principal attraction is the presents sent to Miss Isadora
One notices above all a 'pigeon-blood' ruby whose size and
    lustre are incomparable
None of the young girls present possesses one that can even be
    compared with it
Elegantly dressed
Skilful detectives blend with the crowd of guests watching
    over this gem and protecting it

IV. *Office*

Radiators and ventilators of liquid air
Twelve telephones and five wireless sets
Wonderful electric filing cabinets containing myriads of
    industrial and scientific dossiers on the most varied concerns
The multi-millionaire doesn't really feel at home unless he's
    in this study
Large windows overlook the park and the town
In the evening mercury vapour lamps shed a soft azure
    glimmer of light
It is from there come the orders to sell and buy that sometimes
    topple exchange rates throughout the world

V. *Girl*

Light dress of crêpe de chine
The young girl
Elegance and wealth
Fawn blonde hair with a string of pearls glimmering in it
A countenance regular and composed which reflects frankness
   and kindness
Her big sea blue almost green eyes are clear and bold
She has a fresh and velvety complexion, a special rosiness that
   seems a prerogative of American girls

VI. *Young Man*

It's the Beau-Brummel of Fifth Avenue
Tie of gold cloth sewn with diamond flowerlets
Suit in metallic cloth pink and violet
Boots of real shark skin each button is a little black pearl
He presents asbestos flannel pyjamas another suit of glass stuff a
    crocodile skin waistcoat
His valet soaps his pieces of gold
He never has anything in his portfolio but new and perfumed
    banknotes

IX. *The Thousand Isles*

In this place the landscape is one of the most beautiful to be
    found in North America
The immense sheet of lake water is a blue that is almost white
Hundreds and hundreds of little green isles float on the calm
    surface of the limpid waters
Delicious cottages made of brightly coloured bricks give this
    landscape the appearance of an enchanted kingdom
Sumptuous dinghys of maple-wood or mahogany elegantly
    decked with flags and covered with multi-coloured awnings
    come and go from one isle to another
Any suggestion of weariness of labour of poverty is absent
    from this gracious setting for millionaires

The sun has disappeared on the horizon of Lake Ontario
The clouds bathe their pleats in the vats of scarlet of purple
    violet and orange
What a beautiful evening murmur Andrée and Frederice
    sitting on the terrace of their medieval castle
And the ten thousand motor-boats reply to their ecstasy

X. *Laboratory*

Visit the conservatory
The thermo-syphon maintains a constant temperature there
The earth is saturated with formic acid manganese and other
    substances which impart a formidable strength to the
    vegetation
From one day to the next leaves sprout flowers bloom fruits
    ripen
The roots thanks to an ingenious device bathe in an electric
    current which assures this monstrous growth
The hail-throwing canons demolish nimbus and cumulus
We return to town across the heath
The morning is dazzling
The sombre purple heathers and the golden broom have not
    yet lost their blooms
The gulls and the mews trace big circles in the light blue of
    the sky

Far-West

I. *Cucumingo*

The Hacienda of San-Bernardino
It is built in the middle of a green valley watered by a
    multitude of little streams coming from the surrounding
    mountains
The roofs are of red tiles under the shade of sycamores and
    laurels

Trout abound in the streams
Uncountable herds browse at liberty on the lush grasslands
The orchards are glutted with fruit pears apples grapes
    pineapples figs oranges
And in the kitchen gardens
The vegetables of the old world grow alongside those of the
    tropical countries

Game abounds in the province
Californian pollack
The cotton-tailed rabbit 'cottontail'
The long-eared hare 'jackass'
Quail turtle-dove partridge
Duck and wild geese
Antelope
It is true that you still meet wild-cat and the rattlesnake
    'rattler'
But there are no longer any puma

V. *Club*

The street although indicated on the official town map is made
  of no more than plank fencing and heaps of screenings
You can only cross by haphazardly jumping the pools of water
  and the potholes
At the end of the unfinished road illuminated by powerful arc
  lamps is the Black Bean Club which is also a matrimonial
  agency
Wearing a cow-boy hat or a cap with ear-flaps
Hard faced
Men get out of their brand-new 60 horse power cars which
  they are trying out they get enrolled consult the photograph
  album
They choose their fiancées who on receipt of a telegram
  embark on the Kaiser-Wilhelm at Cherbourg and arrive at
  full-steam
These are mostly Germans
A stable boy dressed in black with felt shoes of icy propriety
  opens the door and surveys the new-comer suspiciously
I drink a whisky cocktail then a second then a third
Then a mint-julep a milk-mother a prairie-osyter a night-cap

VI. *Squaw-Wigwam*

When you have passed through the worm-eaten door made of
    planks torn from packing cases and hinged with scraps of
    leather
You find yourself in a low hall
Smokey
Smell of rotten fish
Stench of fat unabashedly rancid

Barbarian trophies
Head-dress of eagle feathers necklaces of puma teeth or bears'
    claws
Bows arrows tomahawks
Moccasins
Bracelets of grain and glass beads
You still see
Scalping knives one or two ancient carbines a flintlock pistol
    elk and reindeer antlers and a whole collection of little
    embroidered tobacco pouches
Plus three very old pipes made of soft stone with reed stems
Eternally bent over the hearth
The hundred-year-old proprietress of this establishment is
    preserved like a ham and gets smoked and rimed and cured
    like her hundred-year-old pipe and the black of her mouth
    and the black hole of her eye

Aleutian Islands

1.

High cliffs against the icy pole winds
In the centre of fertile grass land
Reindeer elk musk-ox
Blue foxes beavers
Streams full of fish
A low beach has been converted into a seal farm
From the cliff tops they gather eider nests containing down
    which is worth a fortune

2.

Vast and solid buildings which shelter quite a few smugglers
Encircle a little garden with its array of all the plants that can
    withstand this rigorous climate
Service-trees pines arctic willows
Flower borders of heather and alpine plants

3.

A bay studded with rocky islands
In groups of five or six the seals warm themselves in the sun
Or stretched out on the sand
They play amongst themselves with a sort of guttural cry like
    a bark
At the side of the Eskimos' hut there is a lean-to where the
    skins are prepared

River

Mississippi

At this point the river is almost as wide as a lake
The sallow muddy waters roll between two marshy banks
Aquatic plants are continued by the acreages of cotton plants
Here and there appear the towns and villages squatting at the
    end of some little bay with their factories with their high
    black chimneys with their long piers which advance quite a
    way into the water on their stakes

Overwhelming heat
The ship's bell rings for lunch
The passengers sport checked suits loud ties waistcoats glowing
    like the blazing cocktails and the corrosive sauces

You see plenty of crocodiles
The young alive and quivering
The big ones their backs capped with greenish moss let
    themselves drift

The luxuriant vegetation announces the approach of the
    tropics
Giant bamboos palms tulip-trees laurels cedars
The river itself has doubled in width
It is all strewn with floating isles which on the boat's approach
    send up clouds of aquatic birds
Steam-boats sail-boats barges launches of all types and huge
    rafts of wood
A yellow vapour rises from the overheated water of the river

Now the crocos frisk about us by the hundreds
You hear the dry snapping of their jaws and you can see quite
    clearly their ferocious little eyes
The passengers amuse themselves shooting at them with
    precision rifles
When a practised marksman succeeds in his tour de force
    killing or mortally wounding a beast
The others throw themselves on him and tear him to pieces
Ferociously
With little cries almost like the wails of a new-born babe

The South

I. *Tampa*

The train comes to a halt
Only two travellers get out on this burning morning at the
    summer's end
Both are dressed in khaki-coloured suits and are wearing pith
    helmets
Each is followed by a black servant whose duty is to carry their
    cases
They both cast the same distracted look on the too white
    houses of the town on the sky that is too blue
The wind raises little swirls of dust and flies torment the two
    mules of the only cab
The driver sleeps with his mouth open

II. *Bunghalow*

The dwelling is small but very comfortable
The floor timbers are supported by bamboo pillars
Climbing vanilla vines spiral all around
Angola Peas
Jasmin
Overhead dazzling magnolias and corollas of coral-trees

The dining room is furnished with the luxury peculiar to the
    Creoles of Carolina
Enormous chunks of ice in yellow marble vases maintain a
    delicious freshness
Silver plate and sparkling crystal
And behind each guest stands a black servant

The guests dally a long time
Stretched out in rocking chairs they abandon themselves to
    this enervating climate
At a sign from his master Old Jupiter brings out from a little
    lacquered chest
A bottle of sherry
A bucket of ice
Lemons
And a box of Havana cigars

Nobody speaks
The sweat glistens on everyone's face
There's not a breath of air
In the distance you can hear the enormous laugh of the bull-frog
    who abounds in these parts

III. *Vomito Negro*

The landscape is no longer enlivened by gardens or forests
It's bare dismal plain where at long intervals grow
A clump of bamboo
A stunted willow
A eucalyptus buckled by the winds
Then there is the marsh
You see these sallow fumes
This grey mist skimming across the ground agitated by a
    perpetual shuddering
Millions of mosquitoes and the yellow effluvium of rot
There are places there where even the blacks themselves can't
    live

On this side the bank is fringed with big mangroves
Their tangled roots which plunge into the mud are covered
    with bunches of poisonous oysters
The mosquitoes and the venomous insects form a thick cloud
    over the stagnating waters
Beside inoffensive bull-frogs you see toads of prodigious size
And the famous coffin-snake which gives chase to its victims
    gambolling like a dog
There are pools swarming with slate-coloured leeches
Hideous scarlet crabs sport about the sleepy caymans
In the passages where the ground is firmer you meet giant ants
Innumerable and voracious
On these rotten waters in this poisonous filth
Bloom flowers of an astonishing perfume and a heady and
    stubborn scent
Dazzling efflorescence of azure of purple
Chrome foliage

Everywhere
The black water is covered in a carpet of flowers which is
    pierced by the flat heads of serpents

I crossed a thicket of big mimosas
They drew aside for me as I passed
They drew aside with a low whistle
For these trees are sensitive almost nervous
In the midst of jalap creepers full of talking corollas
The big grey and red waders regale themselves on crusty
    lizards and take flight with a great flapping noise at our
    approach
Then there are immense butterflies the colours of sulphur of
    gentian of heavy oil
And sizable caterpillars

IV. *Spanish Ruin*

The nave is in the XVIIIth-century Spanish style
It's all cracked
The damp vault is white with saltpetre and still has some traces
    of gold-leaf
The lantern beams light up a mildewed painting in the corner
It's a Black Virgin
Long mosses and poisonous striped dotted beaded mushrooms
    cover the paving-stones of the sanctuary
There is also a bell with some Latin inscriptions

V. *Golden Gate*

It's the old metal grating that gave the house its name
Bars of iron as thick as your wrist separate the saloon from the
counter where liquors and spirits from everywhere under the
sun stand in rows
In the time when the gold-lust was raging
Where the women brought by the traders from Chile or
Mexico were readily put up for auction
All the bars were equipped with similar grilles
Then the barmen only served their clients with a revolver in
their hands
It wasn't rare for a man to be killed for a drink
It's true that the grillwork is only there now to make it
picturesque
All the same the Chinese are there and drinking
Germans and Mexicans
And also some Canaks arrived with the little steamers loaded
with mother of pearl copra tortoise-shell
Lady singers
Atrocious make-up bank employees bandits sailors with huge
hands

VI. *Oyster Bay*

Canvas tent and bamboo chairs
Every now and again on these deserted beaches you can see a hut
    covered with palm leaves or the skiff of a negro pearl diver

Now the landscape has changed entirely
As far as the eye can see
The beaches are covered with glittering sand
Two or three sharks sport in the wake of the yacht
Florida slips below the horizon

You take a golden regalia from the ebony furniture
You break the end off with the fingernail
You light it voluptuously
Smoke smoke smoke the smoke spirals away

The North

I. *Spring*

The Canadian spring has a vigour and force that one doesn't
  find in any other country of the world
Under the thick layer of snow and ice
Suddenly
Generous nature
Tufts of white blue and pink violets
Orchids sunflowers tiger-lilies
In the venerable avenues of maples of black ash and birches
The birds fly and sing
In the coppice dressed with new and tender buds and shoots
The happy sun is the colour of liquorice

Woods and fields stretch at the side of the road for over five
  miles
It is one of the largest estates in the district of Winnipeg
In the middle rises a solidly constructed farmhouse which has
  the air of a gentleman's residence
My good friend Coulon lives there
Up before daybreak he rides from farm to farm mounted on a
  tall light-bay mare
The paws of his hare-skin cap float on his shoulders
Black eye and bushy eyebrows
All sprightly
Pipe on his chin

The night is misty and cold
A furious west wind makes the elastic pines and the larches
  groan

A little glimmer continues growing
A brazier crackles
The conflagration which was smouldering devours the thickets
    and twigs
The tumultuous wind brings bouquets of resinous trees
One after another
Immense torches burst into flame
The conflagration turns around the horizon with an imposing
    slowness
White trunks and black trunks covered in blood
A dome of chocolate smoke where a million sparks sparklets
    spurt and whirl very high and very low
Behind this curtain of flame you catch sight of big shadows
    which writhe and collapse
Axe blows echo
A misty acre extends over the incandescent forest which the
    team of lumbermen limit

II. *Country*

Magnificent landscape
Verdant forests of pines beech chestnuts broken up by
    flourishing cultures of corn oats buckwheat hemp
Everything breathes abundance
Moreover the country is absolutely deserted
At the most you'll meet here or there a peasant driving a
    cartload of fodder
In the distance the birches rise like columns of silver

III. *Hunting and Fishing*

Wild duck pintail teal geese peewit bustard
Grouse thrushes
Arctic hares snow partridge ptarmigan
Salmon rainbow trout eels
Gigantic pike and crayfish of a particularly exquisite flavour

A rifle slung across the shoulder
Bowie knife in the belt
The hunter and red-skin bend under the weight of game
A rosary of pigeons and red-legged partridge
Wild peacocks
Turkey cocks from the prairies
And even a big reddish white eagle that comes down from the
   clouds

IV. *Harvest*

One six-cylinder and two Fords in the middle of the fields
From all sides and as far as the horizon the lightly inclined
    swathes trace a chequer-board of hesitant lozenges
Not a single tree
From the North comes the racket of the threshers and hay
    carts
And from the South climb the twelve empty trains come to
    carry the wheat

Isles

I. *Victuals*

The little port is very lively this morning
The coolies – Tagals Chinese Malays busily unload a big junk
    with a gilded poop and with sails of plaited bamboo
The cargo consists of porcelain from the big island of Nippon
Swallows' nests gathered in the caves of Sumatra
Sea slugs
Ginger jam
Bamboo shoots in vinegar
All the traders are in a flutter
Mr Noghi pretentiously dressed in a checked suit of American
    manufacture speaks fluent English
It is in this language that these gentlemen carry on their
    discussions
Japanese Canaks Tahitians Papuans Maoris and Fijians

II. *Prospectus*

Visit our island
It is the most southerly isle of the Japanese possessions
Our country is certainly too little known in Europe
It merits attention
The fauna and flora are extremely varied and have hardly been
  studied up until now
Finally you will find picturesque view points everywhere
And in the interior
Ruins of Buddhist temples which are pure marvels of their
  kind

III. *The Red-Crested Viper*

He gives several injections of Dr Yersin serum with the
  hypodermic
Then he enlarges the wound in the arm making a crucial
  incision with his scalpel
He bleeds the wound
Then he cauterizes it with drops of sodium hypochlorite

IV. *Japanese House*

Bamboo canes
Light planks
Paper stretched over the frame
There is no serious means of heating

V. *Little Garden*

Lilies chrysanthemums
Cyclamen and banana trees
Cherries in flower
Palms orange trees and superb coconut palms loaded with
    fruit

VI. *Rock-Garden*

In a basin full of Chinese dolphins and fish with monstrous
  mouths
Some wear little silver rings in their gills

VIII. *Keepsake*

The sky and the sea
The waves caress the roots of the coconut palms and of the big
    tamarinds with metallic leaves

IX. *Bay Full of Fish*

The water is so transparent and so calm
You perceive in the depths the white bush of coral
The prismatic wavering of suspended jellyfish
The flights of fish yellow pink lilac
And at the feet of sinuous algae sky blue sea slugs green and
    violet sea urchins

X. *Hatouara*

She doesn't know of European fashions
Frizzy and bluish black her hair is tied up in the Japanese
   fashion and held by pins of coral
She is naked under her silk kimono
Naked to the elbows

Strong lips
Languorous eyes
Straight nose
Bronzed complexion of clear copper
Slender breasts
Opulent hips

There is in her a vivacity and frankness of movement and
   gesture
The young look of a charming animal

Her science: the grammar of her gait

She swims like one writes a 400 page novel
Tireless
Haughty
Free and easy
Good sustained prose
She captures some tiny little fish which she puts in the hollow
   of her mouth
Then she dives fearlessly
Then she threads between the coral and the multi-coloured
   seaweeds
To reappear soon at the surface

Smiling
Holding in her hand two fat bream with silver stomachs

All proud of her new blue-silk dress her Turkish slippers
    adorned with gold and pretty necklace of coral that has just
    been given to her this very morning
She brings me a basket of weird spiny crabs and huge prawns
    from the tropical seas which are called 'caraques' and are as
    long as your hand

XI. *Softened*

Garden thickly wooded like a glade
On the bank the eternal rustling song of the wind idles in the
    leaves of the filaos
Wearing a light rattan hat armed with a big paper parasol
I contemplate the games of the gulls and the cormorants
Or I examine a flower
Or some stone
At each gesture I frighten the squirrels and the palm rats

By the open window I see the lengthy hull of a steamer of
    medium tonnage
Anchored about two miles off the coast it's already surrounded
    by junks sampans and boats charged with fruit and local
    merchandise
Finally the sun goes down

The air is of a crystalline purity
The same nightingales warble away
And the big vampire bats pass silently in front of the moon on
    their velvet wings

A young girl goes by completely naked
Her head covered by one of those ancient helmets which today
    is the delight of collectors
In her hand she holds a big bouquet of pale flowers of a
    penetrating scent which reminds me of both tuberose and
    narcissus
She stops short in front of the garden gate
Phosphorescent flies have come to settle on the horn which
    tops her helmet and add yet again to the fantastic appearance

Distant nocturnal rumours
Dead branches which break
Sighs of rutting animals
Creepings
Humming of insects
Birds in nests
Whispered voices

The giant plane-trees are pale grey underneath the moon
From the top of their arched roof light lianas fall back an
    invisible mouth sways them in the breeze

Stars dissolve like sugar

River

Bahr-el-Zeraf

There are no tall grasses along the banks
The big expanses of flat land fade away in the distance
The islands are level with the surface of the water
Big crocos warm themselves in the sun
Thousands of big birds cover the banks of sand or mud

The country changes
Now there is quite light bushland dotted with rickety trees
There are delightfully coloured little birds and flights of
    guinea-fowl
In the evening one hears the repeated roars of a lion whose
    silhouette you catch sight of on the west bank
This morning I killed a big scaly lizard a metre and a half long
Always the same landscape of flooded plains
The Arab pilot saw some elephants
There is a big stir
Everyone goes up to the top deck
For each one of us it is the first time that the emperor of the
    animals is about to show himself
The elephants are about three hundred metres off you can see
    two big ones one medium three or four little ones
During lunch someone points out ten huge hippo heads they
    are swimming in front of us

The thermometer hardly varies
Around two o'clock it's regularly between 33 and 38
Clothes are khaki suits and good shoes gaiters and no shirt

We do justice to the ship's fine cuisine and the bottles of
    brown Turin
In the evening one simply adds a white jacket
Kites and vultures pass brushing us lightly with their wings

After dinner the boat steers into mid-stream in order to avoid
    the mosquitoes as much as possible
The banks stretch out covered with papyrus and giant spurge
The journey is slow following the bends of the river
You see plenty of antelopes and gazelles that hardly seem wild
    at all
Now and then an old buffalo but no rhinoceros

Elephant Hunt

I

Infernal terrain
Tall forest rising from marsh with a tangle of lianas and an
    underlevel of low palms with leaves of enormous diameter
Quills straight
About half-past twelve we hear a herd of the big animals we're
    looking for
You lose balance at each moment
The approach is slow
I'd hardly caught sight of the elephants when they took to
    their heels

II

Night
There are elephants in the plantations
The strident noise of branches broken ripped off is succeeded
    by the duller noise of big banana trees turned over with a
    slow push
We are coming right up on them
Climbing a small mound I see the front of the nearest animal
The moon is directly overhead the light favourable it's a
    handsome elephant
The trunk in the air the end turned towards me
He's caught my scent there's not a half-second to lose
The shot fired
Immediately a new bullet goes into the Winchester's breech
Then I smoke my pipe
The huge animal seems to sleep in the blue glade

III

We arrive in clay country
After their mud bath the animals went through some
    particularly heavy thickets
At fifteen metres one can only make out vague masses so that
    it's impossible to get any idea of either their size or tusks
I've rarely heard so clearly the intestinal noises of the elephants
    their snorting the noise of branches breaking
All that comes after long silences during which you'd find it
    hard to believe they were so near

IV

From the camp we can hear the elephants in the forest
I keep a man with me to carry the big Kodak
At twelve metres I can hardly make out a big animal
I think I can see a little one next to her
They're in the swamp water
I can literally hear them gargling
The sun shines right down on the head and breast of the large
    female now irritated
What an interesting photo the cool-headed man beside me was
    able to take

V

The terrain is impossible
Passable only if you follow the paths made by the elephants
    themselves
Paths littered with obstacles inverted tree trunks
Lianas these powerful animals step over or simply brush aside
    with their trunks
Without ever breaking them or pushing them down so they'll
    never be in the way again

They are like the natives who never remove obstacles either
    not even on the most beaten tracks

VI

We cut across the trail of a big male again
The animal leads us due west right across the great plain
Goes through five hundred metres of forest
Circles awhile in an uncovered space we hadn't known about
Then back into the forest
Now the animal is perfectly still only a snort gives him away
    from time to time
At ten metres I can vaguely see something
Can it be him?
Yes look a big white tooth
At this moment torrential rain and black obscurity start to fall
The film is ruined

VII

Sometimes the elephant trails snake and criss-cross
Hemmed in between walls of thorny bushes
That vegetation is impenetrable even for the eyes
It's from three to six metres high
Along the tracks the lianas fall as far as one two three feet
    from the ground
Then climb up again assuming the most bizarre shapes
The trees are all enormous the collar of their aerial roots is
    from four to five metres from the ground

VIII

We hear a herd
It's in the clearing
The grass and undergrowth grow five or six metres high

There are also limited bare spaces
I have my three men stay each one aiming his Bell-Howell
And I go forward alone with my little Kodak on ground
     where I can walk quietly
There is nothing funnier than to see the elephants' trunks
Twisting in every direction going up down up again
While the head and whole immense body remain hidden

IX

I approach in a semi-circle
Raising his enormous head embellished with big tusks
Mashing the air with his wide ears
The trunk turned towards me
He sniffs the wind
A photo and a bullet are shot
The elephant takes the shock without flinching
I do it again very quickly
Stung in the head he rolls on the ground with a tremendous
     death rattle
Then I fire a bullet towards the heart and then two shots in the
     head
The rattle is still powerful but finally life abandons him
I noted the position of the heart and its dimensions which are
     55 centimetres diameter by 40

X

I see the handsome animal just for an instant
Now I hear his regular splashing
He crumples the branches in his way
It's a grandiose music
He is up against me and I can't see a thing
Suddenly his huge head breaks through the undergrowth
Full face

At six metres
Right over me
The elephant does a quick back step
At that moment the rain began to fall with a din that stifled
    the noise of his strides

XI

On a big plain to the north
At the skirt of the forest a large female and a little male and
    three young elephants of different sizes
The height of the grass prevents me from photographing them
From the top of an ant-heap I watch them for a long time
    with my Zeiss binoculars
The elephants seem to be taking their dessert with an amusing
    delicacy of touch
When the animals scent us they clear out
The bush opens up to make way for them and closes again
    like a curtain over their giant forms

Menus

I

Green turtle liver with truffles
Lobster à la Mexicaine
Florida pheasant
Caribbean iguana sauce
Gombos and cabbage-palm

II

Red Rio salmon
Canadian bear ham
Minnesota prairie roast beef
Smoked eels
Tomatoes from San Francisco
Pale ale and wines from California

III

Salmon from Winnipeg
Scots ham of mutton
Royal Canadian apples
Old French wines

IV

Kankal oysters
Lobster salad celery hearts
Vanillad French snails in sugar
Kentucky chicken
Dessert coffee Canadian-Club whisky

V

Shark fins pickled in brine
Young still-born dogs prepared in honey
Rice wine with violets
Creamed silk-worm cocoons
Salty earthworms and alcohol from Kawa
Seaweed jam

VI

Tins of Chicago beef and German salted meats
Crayfish
Pineapples guavas loquats coconut mangoes apple-cream
Baked bread fruit

VII

Turtle soup
Fried oysters
Bears paw with truffles
Spiny Javanese lobster

VIII

River-crab stew with red peppers
Sucking pig surrounded by fried bananas
Hedgehog ravensara
Fruit

Travelling 1887–1923

from

Travel Warrant

I. *Formosa*

Waking

I always sleep with the windows open
I slept like a man alone
The sirens and hooters hadn't woken me too often

This morning I am leaning out of the window
I see
The sky
The sea
The landing stage where I arrived from New York in 1911
The pilot boat
And
To the left
The smoke stacks the cranes the arc lamps against the light
The first tram shivers in the icy dawn
Me I'm too hot
Good-bye Paris
Hello sunshine

You are More Beautiful Than the Sky and the Sea

When you love you must leave
Leave your wife leave your child
Leave your friend leave your girlfriend
Leave your mistress leave your lover
When you love you must leave

The world is full of Negroes and Negresses
Of men and women and men and women
Look at the fine shops
This taxi this man that woman that taxi
And all the fine goods

There is the air there is the wind
The mountains the waters the sky the earth
The children the animals
The plants and the coals of earth

Learn to sell to buy to re-sell
Give take give take
When you love you must know
How to sing run eat drink
Whistle
And learn to work

When you love you must leave
Don't whimper as you smile
Don't hide between her breasts
Breathe get up and go

I take my bath and I look
I see the mouth I know
The hand the leg The the eye
I take my bath and I look

The whole world is always there
Life is full of extraordinary things
I leave the chemist
I just step off the scales
I'm 80 kilos
I love you

En Route for Dakar

The air is cold
The sea is made of steel
The sky is cold
My body is made of steel
Good-bye Europe which I'm leaving for the first time since
 1914
Nothing about you interests me any more not even the
 emigrants on the lower deck Jews Russians Basques Spaniards
 Portuguese and German buffoons who yearn for Paris
I want to forget everything and never speak your languages
 again and sleep with Negroes Negresses Indians animals and
 plants
And bathe and live in the sun
 in the company of a big banana tree
And love the fat bud of this plant
To segment myself
To become as hard as a pebble
To fall in the nick of time
And sink to the depths

35° 57' Latitude North
15° 16' Longitude West

Today it happened
I'd been awaiting the event since the crossing began
The sea was fine with a heavy ground-swell that made us roll
The sky had been clouded over since morning
It was four in the afternoon
I was busy playing dominoes
Suddenly I gave a cry and ran up to the bridge
It's happened it's happened
Ultramarine blue
The blue topgallant sail of the sky
The atmosphere was hot
One just doesn't know how this happened or how to define
   this thing
But everything mounted one degree in tonality
(This was as clear as two and two make four)
By now the sky was clear
The sun went down like a wheel
The moon came up like another wheel
The stars became bigger and bigger

This point is found between Madeira on the starboard and
   Casablanca on the port-side
Already

In Sight of the Isle of Fuerteventura

Everything has magnified yet again since yesterday
The water the sky the purity of the atmosphere
The Canary Isles look like the banks of Lake Como
The trails of clouds are like glaciers
It begins to get hot

On Board Formosa

The sky is black ribbed with leprous bands
The water is black
The stars grow even bigger and melt like lachrymose candles
This is what happens on board

On the fo'c'sle four Russians are installed in a bundle of rope
    and play cards in the glimmer of a Venetian lantern

On the front deck the Jews a minority like back home in
    Poland huddle together and give way to the Spaniards who
    play the mandolin singing and dancing La Jota

In the superstructure the Portuguese emigrants dance a peasant
    round a black man clacks two long bone castanets and the
    couples break the round revolving and returning tapping
    their heels while a woman's shrill voice rises

The first class passengers look on nearly all of them and envy
    these popular games

In the saloon a pretentious German woman plays the violin
    with plenty of chichi with plenty of chichi
    a pretentious young French woman
    accompanies her on the piano

On the promenade deck a mysterious Russian officer of the
    Grand Duke's guard comes and goes incognito Dostoevskian
    personality whom I have baptized Dobro Vetcher he's a
    sad little fellow this evening he is taken with a certain
    nervous agitation he's wearing patent leather pumps a
    Basque coat and a huge bowler like my father in his 1895
    portrait

In the smoking room people are playing dominoes a young
doctor who looks like Jules Romains and who is on his way
to the High Sudan a Belgian arms manufacturer who will
debark at Pernambuco a Dutchman his forehead cut in two
hemispheres by a deep scar he is the director of the
Mount-of-Piety of Santiago in Chile and a little plebian
ragamuffin actress from Ménilmontant who knows a few
tricks in the motor trade she even offers me a lead mine in
Brazil and an oil well in Bakou

On the rear deck the German immigrants clean and
painstakingly well-groomed sing with their wives and
children hard hymns and sentimental songs

On the back bridge everyone argues very loudly and squabbles
in all the Eastern European languages

In the steward's room the people from Bordeaux play manille
and at his station the wireless operator curses Santander and
Mogador

Artificial Eggs

While waiting to go ashore we drink cocktails in the smoking
    room
A banker tells us about the installation and functioning of an
    artificial egg factory established in a Bordeaux suburb
They make the white of the egg with the haemoglobin of
    horses' blood
The yoke is made of very impalpable cornflower and fine oils
This mixture is poured into round moulds which are then
    frozen
Thus a yellow ball is obtained which is then dipped in coliure
    so that a thin film forms around it
This product is coated with whipped haemoglobin and then
    the whole lot is returned to the fridge where the white of
    the egg will set on being exposed to a very low temperature
A new bath in coliure then one obtains by a very simple
    process a calcareous precipitation which forms the shell
This reminds me of something I saw before the war in
    Düsseldorf machines for polishing mellowing and blending
    coffee grains
Thus giving poor quality coffee the appearance of coffee beans
    from Jamaica Bourbon Borneo Arabia etc

Sunsets

Everybody talks of sunsets
All the travellers are in agreement in talking about the sunsets
  in these parts
There are plenty of old books where nothing is described but
  sunsets
Tropical sunsets
Yes it's true they're splendid
But I prefer the sunrise by far
The dawn
I never miss one
I am always on the bridge
Naked
And I am always alone in my admiration
But I am not going to describe the dawn
I am going to keep it for myself

Starry Nights

I pass most of the night on the bridge
The familiar stars of our latitude decline decline on the sky
The Pole star descends more and more on the northern horizon
Orion – my constellation – is at its zenith
The Milky Way like a luminous crevice enlarges each night
The Big Dipper is a little mist
The south is blacker and blacker in front of us
And I await impatiently the appearance of the Southern Cross in
    the east
To give me patience Venus has doubled in size and quintupled
    in brilliance like the moon she makes a trail on the sea
Tonight I saw a meteor fall

White Suit

I walk on the bridge in my white suit that I bought in Dakar
On my feet my rope sandals bought at Villa Garcia
In my hand my Basque cap brought back from Biarritz
My pockets are full of Caporals Ordinaires
From time to time I sniff my little wooden box from Russia
I jingle the small change in my pocket and a pound sterling in
    gold
I have my big Calabrian handkerchief and these wax matches
    of a size you don't find anywhere but in London
I am clean washed scrubbed more than the deck
Happy as a king
Rich as a millionaire
Free as a man

Baggage

Say that people travel with heaps of baggage
Me I only took my cabin trunk and already I find that it's too
    much I've too many things
This is what my trunk contains
The manuscript of Moravagine which I must finish on board
    and post in Santos to dispatch it to Grasset
The manuscript of Plan de l'Aiguille which I must finish as
    soon as possible in order to dispatch to Sans Pareil
The manuscript of a ballet for the next season of the Swedish
    Ballet which I did on board between Le Havre and La Pallice
    where I sent it to Satie
The manuscript of Coeur du Monde which I'll send bit by bit
    to Raymone
The manuscript of Equatoria
A big batch of Negro stories which forms the second volume
    of my anthology
Several business dossiers
The two bulky volumes of the dictionary Darmesteter
My Remington Portable latest model
A packet containing little things which I must send back to a
    woman in Rio
My Turkish slippers from Timbuctoo which bear the trademark
    of the big caravan
Two pairs of mythical boots
One pair of patent leather
Two suits
Two overcoats
My big Mont-Blanc sweater
Some small toilet articles
One tie

Six dozen handkerchiefs
Three night shirts
Six pairs of pyjamas
Kilos of white paper
Kilos of white paper
And a JuJu
My trunk weighs 57 kilos without my grey hat

S. Fernando de Noronha

I send a telegram to Santos to announce my arrival
Then I go back up and get in the swimming pool
As I was swimming on my back and playing at whales Mr
   Sheep the ship's radio telegraph officer announces to me that
   he is in communication with 'Belle-Isle' and asks me if I
   wouldn't like to send an ocean-letter (to Madame Raymone
   he adds with a beautiful smile)
I send an ocean-letter to say that it's a good life
And get back in the water
The water is cool
The water is salty

Sunday

It's Sunday at sea
It's hot
I'm closed in my cabin as if in melting butter

Rio de Janeiro

Everyone is up on deck
We are in the middle of the mountains
A lighthouse goes out
You look everywhere for the Sugar-Loaf and ten people
    discover it at once in a hundred different directions these
    mountains look so alike in their pear-shaped forms
M. Lopart shows me a mountain whose profile on the sky is
    like a stretched out corpse and whose silhouette looks very
    much like that of Napoleon on his death-bed
I find that it looks more like Wagner a Richard Wagner
    puffed up with pride or flooded with grease
Rio is close by now and you can make out the houses on the
    beach
The officers compare this panorama with the Golden Horn
Others tell the story of the revolt of the fort
Others unaminously regret the construction of a huge modern
    hotel high and square which disfigures the bay (it's very
    beautiful)
Others again protest vehemently at the abrasion of a mountain
Leant over the starboard bulwarks I gaze at
The tropical vegetation of an abandoned isle
The big sun which ploughs the big vegetation
A little boat manned by three fishermen
These men with slow methodical movements
Who work
Who fish
Who haul in their catch
Who don't even look at us
Totally at their work

Dead of Night at Sea

The mountainous coast is illuminated at giorno by the full
    moon which travels with us
The Southern Cross is in the east and the south remains in
    total darkness
The heat is suffocating
Big pieces of wood swim in the opaque water
The two German acrobats walk about on the bridge three-
    quarters naked
They are trying to cool off
The little Portuguese doctor who accompanies his country's
    emigrants as far as Buenos-Aires winks as he passes in front
    of me
I see him swallowed up with the two Germans in a big
    unoccupied cabin
Two ships pass on the starboard side then three on the port
    side
All five are lit up like a carnival
You could imagine you were in the port at Monte-Carlo and
    the virgin forest grows down to the sea
Pricking up my ears and straining all my attention I hear
    something like the rustling of the leaves
Or perhaps my grief at leaving the ship tomorrow
At the end of a long quarter of an hour I hear the thin song of
    an emigrant on the front deck where the linen dries by the
    moon and makes signs at me

Paris

I stayed up all night on the bridge listening to the messages
    which came over the wireless decoding several fragments
And translating them winking at the stars
A new star shone at nose level
The embers of my cigar
I was dreaming absent-mindedly of Paris
And each star of the sky was replaced every now and then by
    a familiar face
I saw Jean like a wanton torch Eric's malicious eye Ferdinand's
    steady look and the eyes of lots of cafés around Sanders
Eugenia's round spectacles and Marcel's
Margaret's glance like an arrow and Gascon's nodding look
From time to time Francis and Germaine passed in a motor-car
    and Abel who was doing stage production and was sad
Then the wireless resumed and I was looking at the stars
And the new star lit up anew at the end of my nose
It lit me up like Raymone
So close so close

Dawn

At dawn I went down in the engines
I listened to the deep breathing of the pistons for the last time
Supported by the fragile nickel hand rail for the last time I
    sensed the dull vibration of the main-shaft penetrating me
    with the mustiness of over-heated oils and the tepidness of
    steam
We drank another glass the chief mechanic this quiet sad man
    who has the beautiful smile of a child and who never talks
    and I
As I left him the sun was coming out of the sea quite
    naturally and its heat was already intense
Not a single cloud in the mauve sky
And as we pointed towards Santos our wake described a big
    arc mirrored on the immobile sea

The Beach Guaruja

It's two o'clock and we're finally at the quayside
I discovered a bunch of people in the shade in the squat
    shadow of a crane
Medical certificates passports customs
I go ashore
I'm not sitting in the car I'm travelling in but in a thick wet
    heat stuffed like the coachwork
My friends who have been waiting for me since seven that
    morning in the sun on the quay still have just enough energy
    to shake my hand
The whole town echoes with the sound of young motor horns
    saluting each other
Young motor horns which re-awaken us
Young motor horns which make us hungry
Young motor horns which take us to lunch at the beach
    Guaruja
In a restaurant full of one-arm bandits electric shooting galleries
    mechanical birds automatic machines which read your palm
    gramophones which tell your fortune and where we eat
    good Brazilian food savoury spiced Negro Indian

Banana Plantation

We take one more ride in the car before taking the train
We cross the dusty banana plantations
The putrid abbatoir
A miserable suburb and the flourishing bush
Then travel along the side of a mountain of red soil where
    there's a drift of square houses daubed with red and dark-
    blue paint wooden houses built up on old abandoned sites
Two dwarfish goats munch the rare plants which grow at the
    side of the road two dwarfish goats and a little blue pig

Landscape

The earth is red
The sky is blue
The vegetation is dark green
This landscape is cruel hard sad in spite of the infinite variety
    of vegetative forms
In spite of the leaning grace of palms dazzling bouquets of big
    trees in flower Lenten flowers

In the Train

The train goes quite fast
The signals points and level crossings work the same as in
  England
Nature is a much darker green than back home
Copper coloured
Closed
The forest has the face of an Indian
Whereas yellow and white dominate in our meadows
Here it's sky blue which colours the flowered plains

Paranapiacaba

The Paranapiacaba is the Sierra do Mar
Here the train is hoisted by cables and crosses over the rugged
    mountain in several sections
All the stations are suspended in the void
There are many waterfalls and they had to undertake great
    works of art to prop up the crumbling mountain
For the Sierra is a rotten mountain like the Rognes above
    Bionnasay but the Rognes covered in tropical forest
The weeds which grow on the embankment in the cutting
    between the rails are all rare plants that you never see in
    Paris except in the windows of big horticulturalists
In one station three indolent half-breeds were hoeing them out

Telegraph Line

You see this telegraph line at the bottom of the valley whose
   rectilinear trail cuts the forest on the mountain opposite
All the poles are iron
When they were installed the poles were wood
At the end of three months branches had sprouted on them
So they tore them out turned them round and replanted them
   the head in the ground the roots in the air
At the end of three months they had grown new branches
   they had taken root again and started to live again
They had to tear them all out and re-establish a new line they
   had to bring iron poles at great expense from Pittsburg

São-Paulo

Finally here are the factories a suburb a pretty little tramline
Electric cables
A populous street with people going about their evening
  shopping
A gasometer
Finally we enter the station
Saint-Paul
I believe I'm in Nice Station
Or getting out at Charing Cross London
I find all my friends
Hello
It's me

Le Havre–Saint-Paul, February 1924

II. *São-Paulo*

Small Fry

The sky is crude blue
The wall opposite is crude white
The crude sun strikes me on the head
A Negress installed on a little terrace fries little tiny fish on a
    jagged stove in an old biscuit tin
Two piccaninnys gnaw a stem of sugar cane

Landscape

The Ripolin enamelled walls of the PENSION MILANESE are
    framed by my window
I see a slice of the avenue Sao-João
Trams cars trams
Trams – trams trams trams
Yellow mules yoked in threes pull little empty carts
Over the pepper trees of the avenue hangs the giant ensign of
    the CASA TOKIO
The sun pours out varnish

Saint-Paul

I adore this town
Saint-Paul is after my own heart
Here no tradition
No prejudice
Neither ancient nor modern
All that counts is this furious appetite this absolute confidence
  this optimism this audacity this work this labour this
  speculation which puts up ten houses an hour in all
  ridiculous styles grotesque beautiful big little north south
  egyptian yankee cubist
Without any other preoccupations than to follow statistics
  forecast the future comfort utility capital appreciation and to
  attract a gross immigration
All countries
All nationalities
I like that
The two or three old portuguese houses which remain are blue
  china

III

Cabin 2

It's mine
It's all white
I'll be very comfortable here
All alone
For I must do a lot of work
To recapture the nine months in the sun
Nine months in Brazil
Nine months with Friends
And I must work for Paris
That's why I already like this crammed boat where I can see
    nobody to have a little chat with

At Table

I had tipped the chief steward well so as to have a little table
    to myself in a corner
I won't make any acquaintances
I look at the others and I eat
Here is the first menu of European taste
I must admit that I enjoy eating these European dishes
Pompadour soup
Rump steak à la Bruxelloise
Young partridge on fried bread
Taste is the most atavistic sense the most reactionary the most
    national
Analytic
At the antipodes of love of touching of touching of love in full
    evolution and universal growth
Revolutionary
Synthetic

Waking

I am naked
I've already had my bath
I rub myself over with Eau de Cologne
A badly buffeted sailing boat passes my port-hole
It's cold this morning
There's mist
I arrange my papers
I work out my timetable
My days will be well filled
There's not a minute to lose
I write

Rio de Janeiro

A dazzling light floods the atmosphere
A light so coloured and so fluid that the objects it touches
The pink rocks
The white lighthouse which towers over them
The semaphore signals seem liquefied in it
And now that I know the names of the mountains which
    surround this marvellous bay
The Sleeping Giant
The Gavea
Le Bico de Papagaio
The Corcovado
The Sugar-Loaf which Jean de Lery's companions call the
    Butter-Pot
And the strange needles of the Chain of Organs
Hello You All

Dinner in Town

Mr Lopart was no longer in Rio he had left on Saturday by
    the 'Lutetia'
I dined in town with the new director
After having signed the contract 24F/N type Grand Sport I took
    him to a little dive on the port
We ate grilled shrimps
Dolphin tongues in mayonnaise
Armadillo
(The armadillo meat tastes like reindeer meat that Satie loves)
Fruit of the country mummys bananas oranges from Bahia
Everyone drank their fiasco de chianti

The Morning Belongs To Me

The sun rises at quarter to six
The wind has freshened a good deal
In the morning the bridge belongs to me until nine
I look at the sailors who sponge the spardeck
The high waves
A Brazilian steamer which we are catching up with
A single and unique bird white and black
When the first women appear the wind buffets them and blows
    about the little girls uncovering their goose-pimpled little
    bottoms and I go back to my cabin
And start work again

Bad Faith

This damned chief-steward even though I've tipped him well
    so as to be left alone has come around like a mangy cat
He begs me on behalf of the captain to come and take a place
    at the head table
I am furious but I cannot refuse
Over dinner it turns out that the captain is quite a congenial
    fellow
I am between an attaché of the embassy at The Hague and an
    English consul from Stockholm
On the other side is a world authority on bacteriology and his
    wife a sweet greedy woman with such white skin and round
    flat eyes
My antimusical paradoxes and my culinary theories throw the
    table into a fluster of indignation
The attaché from The Hague dips his monocle in the broth
The consul from Stockholm turns a congested green like a
    striped pyjama
The world authority on bacteriology lengthens yet again his
    pointed ferrety head
His wife clucks and wrinkles from the centre to the periphery
    so well that her face finally looks like a fat man's navel
The captain gives a malicious wink

Smoking

It's only the shabby who haven't a smoking jacket on board
Only too-well-brought-up people have smoking jackets on
    board
I put on a little suit of English Cheviot and the sea is as even a
    blue as my blue tropical suit

Night Rises

I carefully observed how this happened
When the sun has gone down
It's the sea that darkens
The sky remains chiefly clear for a good while longer
The night climbs up through the water and slowly encircles
    the whole horizon
Then the sky darkens slowly in its turn
There is a moment when it becomes completely black
Then the black of the water and the black of the sky recede
There settles an eburnean transparence with the reflections in
    the water and in the obscured pockets in the sky
Then the Sack of Coal under the Southern Cross
Then the Milky Way

Bahia

Lagoons churches palms cubical houses
Big boats with two reversed rectangular sails which look like
    two huge trouser legs filled with wind
Skiffs with shark's fins which leap through the ground swell
Big perpendicular clouds swollen and coloured like pottery
Yellow and blue

Sharks

Someone calls me
There are sharks in our wake
Two three monsters which leap slewing through the foam
    when you throw them chickens
I buy a sheep which I sling overboard
The sheep swims the sharks are afraid I've been cheated

A Line

A line which blurs
Good-bye
It's America
Above it a crown of clouds
In the coming night a star of the first water
Now we are going to sail east and from tomorrow the
    swimming pool will be in operation on the upper deck

Laughter

I laugh
I laugh
You laugh
We laugh
Nothing matters anymore
Save this laughter that we love
It's necessary to know how to be stupid and happy

Peak

There is a peak and no one could tell me its name
It looks like the Matterhorn and it's the last pillar of Atlantis
What a thrill when I think I'm about to discover in the
　　telescope the traces of an Atlantine terrace

Civilization

There are some traces of cultivation
Some houses
A radio station two pylons and two Eiffel towers under
  construction
An old Portuguese port
A calvary
In the telescope I can make out a naked man on the wall of
  the prison waving a white rag
The nights are most beautiful without a moon with immense
  stars and the heat which does nothing but grow
As the turning of the propellers makes the night water more
  and more phosphorescent in our wake

Passengers

They are all there sitting in deck chairs
Or playing cards
Or taking tea
Or being bored
All the same there's a little group of sportsmen playing
    shuffle-board
Or deck tennis
And another little group who are going to swim in the pool
At night when everyone is asleep the rows of empty chairs
    along the deck are like a collection of skeletons in a museum
Old dried up women
Chameleons dandruff nails

Wash

The sea continues to be this sea blue
The weather continues to be the finest weather I've ever known
  at sea
This crossing continues to be the most calm and most devoid
  of incident that one could ever imagine

Ball

An American couple dance Apache dances
The young Argentinians pout at the orchestra and cordially
    scorn the young people on board
The Portuguese burst into applause when they play a
    Portuguese tune
The French keep to themselves and laugh loudly and mock
    everyone
Only the little maids want to dance in their pretty dresses
I invite the Negro wet nurse to dance to the great scandal of
    some and to the amusement of others
The American couple dance Apache dances again

South Americans

I

The road climbs in loops
The car goes abruptly and powerfully
We climb with the roar of an aeroplane that's going to reach
    ceiling
Each spiral throws her against my shoulder and when we turn
    in the void she clings obliviously to my arm and leans over
    the precipice
At the top of the sierra we stop short in front of a giant rift
Close by a monstrous moon climbs up behind us
'Lua, Lua!' she murmurs
In the name of the moon, my friend, how does God authorize
    these gigantic works which allowed us to cross
It's not the moon, darling, but the sun which by precipitating
    the fogs created this enormous rent
Look at the water which runs at the bottom amongst the
    débris of the mountains and is engulfed in the shafts of the
    factory
This station sends electricity as far as Rio

II

Libertines and free-thinkers
Now we can admit
There aren't many of us in the world
Integral health
We also have the most beautiful women in the world
Simplicity
Intelligence
Love

Sports
We have also taught them liberty
The children grow up with dogs and horses and birds in the
    midst of pretty servants all round and mobile like sunflowers

III

There is no more jealousy or fear or timidity
Our girl friends are sound and sane
They are beautiful and simple and big
They all know how to dress
These aren't intelligent women but they're all very shrewd
They're not frightened of loving
They're not afraid to take
They all know just as well how to give
Each one of them has had to contend with her family their
    position people or other things
Now
They have simplified their lives and are full of childishness
No more furniture no more trinkets they love animals big cars
    and their smiles
They travel
They detest music but they always take a gramophone with
    them

IV

There are three that I love particularly
The first
An old lady sensitive beautiful and good
An adorable chatterer of supreme elegance
A society woman but full of such gluttony that she has freed
    herself of worldliness
The second is the wild girl of the Hotel Maurice
All day she combs her long hair and gnaws her Guerlain rouge

144

Banana trees Negro wet nurses humming birds
Her country is so far away that one must travel six weeks on a
    river covered in flowering mosses and mushrooms as big as
    ostrich eggs
She is so beautiful in the evening in the entrance hall of the
    hotel that all the men are mad about her
Her most shrill smile is for me for I know how to laugh like
    the wild bees of her country
The last is too rich to be happy
But she has already made great progress
It's not at the first attempt that you can find your balance and
    simplicity of life amongst all the complications of being rich
One must be stubborn
She knows it well she who rides a horse so divinely and makes
    such a fine figure with her grand Argentinian stallion
Let your will be your whip
But don't use it
Too
Often

v

There is yet another who is still like a little girl
In spite of her horrible husband her frightful divorce and being
    shut away in a convent
She's as shy as day and night
She is more beautiful than an egg
More beautiful than a circle
But she is always too naked her beauty overflows she doesn't
    yet know how to dress
She also eats far too much and her stomach swells as if she
    were two months pregnant
She has such an appetite and such a lust for life
We are going to teach her all this and teach her how to dress
And give her good addresses

VI

One
There is another
One whom I love more than anything in the world
I give myself to her completely like a Pepsin for she needs a
    tonic
For she is too sweet
For she is still a bit timid
For happiness is a heavy thing to carry
For beauty needs a quarter of an hour's exercise every morning

VII

We don't want to be sad
It's too easy
It's too stupid
It's too convenient
One has the opportunity too often
It's not so clever
Everyone is sad
We don't want to be sad anymore

from

Diverse Poems

Homage to Guillaume Apollinaire

The bread rises
France
Paris
A whole generation
I address the poets who were present
Friends
Apollinaire is not dead
You have followed an empty hearse
Apollinaire is a seer
It's he who was smiling in the silk of the flags at the window
He was amusing himself throwing flowers and crowns at you
While you were going by behind his hearse
Then he bought a little tri-coloured cockade
I saw him the same evening demonstrating in the boulevards
He was astride the bonnet of an American truck and
    brandished an enormous international flag flying like an
    aeroplane
VIVE LA FRANCE

Time passes
The years slip away like clouds
The soldiers have gone back
To their homes
To their countries
And so a new generation grows up
The dream of MAMMALS is realized
Little Frenchmen, part English, part Negro, part Russian, a
    little Belgian, Italian, Annamite, Czech
One with a Canadian accent, the other with Hindoo eyes
Teeth face bones joints figure gait and smile

They've all got something foreign about them and yet they
    come from here
In the midst of them Apollinaire, like that statue of the Nile,
    spread out, father of the waters, with little kids running
    about him everywhere
Between his feet, under his armpits, in his beard
They look like their father and go from him
And they all speak the language of Apollinaire

Paris, November 1918

Leaving Paris

Bébé Cadum wishes you bon voyage
Thank you, Michelin, for when I return
Like the Negro fetishes in the bush
The petrol pumps are naked

More About Penguins
and Pelicans

Penguinews, which appears every month, contains details of all the new books issued by Penguins as they are published. It is supplemented by our stocklist, which includes almost 5,000 titles.

A specimen copy of *Penguinews* will be sent to you free on request. Please write to Dept EP, Penguin Books Ltd, Harmondsworth, Middlesex, for your copy.

In the U.S.A.: For a complete list of books available from Penguins in the United States write to Dept CS, Penguin Books, 625 Madison Avenue, New York, New York 10022.

In Canada: For a complete list of books available from Penguins in Canada write to Penguin Books Canada Ltd, 2801 John Street, Markham, Ontario L3R 1B4.

In Australia: For a complete list of books available from Penguins in Australia write to the Marketing Department, Penguin Books Australia Ltd, P.O. Box 257, Ringwood, Victoria 3134.

Penguin Modern European Poets

This series includes work by the following poets, in verse
translations by, among others, W.H. Auden, Lawrence Ferlinghetti,
Michael Hamburger, Ted Hughes, J.B. Leishman and Christopher
Middleton:

Amichai	Mandelstam
Blok	Pavese
Césaire	Rilke
Ekelöf	Yevtushenko

Penguin Modern European Poets

RENGA

A Chain of Poems by Octavio Paz, Jacques Roubaud, Edoardo
Sanguinetti and Charles Tomlinson

Edited by Charles Tomlinson

Based on the principle of the Japanese *renga* – a sequence of linked
poems – this remarkable composition is the work of four poets of
international stature: Octavio Paz; Jacques Roubaud; Edoardo
Sanguinetti and Charles Tomlinson

'*Renga*' said *The Times Literary Supplement* when it was published
in France 'is a very significant book, appealing with a particular
force to anyone who suspects that English poetry could do with a
major renewal . . . It is a work of great beauty and of possibly
seminal importance . . . It concentrates the internationalization of
poetry. It is an education in reading . . . It is a new genre.'

Published now for the first time in Britain, this multilingual poem
appears with Charles Tomlinson's English translation on facing
pages.

OCTAVIO PAZ

Selected Poems

A bilingual edition edited by Charles Tomlinson

Born in 1914 in Mexico, Octavio Paz, a dazzling and mercurial
writer equally at home with French Surrealism, American poetry,
German Romanticism and Marxist polemic, is now clearly established
as one of Latin America's greatest poets.

The struggle to integrate his multiple personae, and to reconcile his
country's past and future with the modern world, dominates much
of his poetry. So too does his self-imposed task of making a
delicate and exact 'literal statement of consciousness' – which he
approaches 'by way of a persistent questioning of all reality'.

Two new Penguin anthologies

THE PENGUIN BOOK OF FIRST WORLD WAR POETRY

Edited by Jon Silkin

This volume offers the best work by the best poets of the war.
A few of them, like Kipling, Hardy and Flint, were not combatants
yet wrote poetry concerned with the War; others, like Edward
Thomas, did not survive long enough for the experience of combat
to enter into their work. But most of the poets were also soldiers
and the representatives of a crucial period in the development of
English poetry.

This anthology also includes a selection (in translation) of
German, French and Italian war poetry.

THE PENGUIN BOOK OF SPANISH CIVIL WAR VERSE

Edited by Valentine Cunningham

This is the first comprehensive assembly of British poems
(some never before published) which have to do with the Spanish
Civil War. It includes also supporting prose reports and reviews
by the poets, and a selection of poems – notably Spanish romanceros
– in translation.

Some of this century's best-known literary figures – Auden, Spender,
McNeice and Orwell among them – are naturally represented, but
the collection also puts firmly on the map the work of several
undeservedly neglected poets, such as Charles Donnelly,
Clive Branson and Miles Tomalin.

Penguin Modern Classics

MORAVAGINE
Blaise Cendrars

'How can I convince the sceptic that I was ravished by Cendrars' *Moravagine*? How does one know immediately that a thing is after one's own heart? . . . some men compel you to accept them, compel you to understand, and finally, to adore' – Henry Miller

Since its first publication in France in 1926, this ferocious and fantastic masterpiece has established itself as a classic of twentieth-century fiction.

The semi–autobiographical story is narrated by a young French doctor who encounters Moravagine in a Swiss lunatic asylum and promptly helps him to escape. Together they travel the world – rally to support the Russian Revolution, narrowly escape being eaten alive by American Blue Indians, and fight in the First World War.

Full of tenderness, horror and savage humour, *Moravagine* is a dazzling piece of writing by one of the founders of the modern movement in literature.